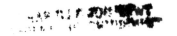

Sacagawea

Jane Sutcliffe

⌐ LERNER PUBLICATIONS COMPANY • MINNEAPOLIS

For Mary Anne

Illustrations by Tad Butler

Text copyright © 2009 by Jane Sutcliffe
Illustrations copyright © 2009 by Lerner Publishing Group, Inc.

Lerner Publications Company
A division of Lerner Publishing Group, Inc.
241 First Avenue North
Minneapolis, MN 55401 U.S.A.

Website address: www.lernerbooks.com

Library of Congress Cataloging-in-Publication Data

Sutcliffe, Jane.
    Sacagawea / by Jane Sutcliffe.
        p.   cm. — (History maker biographies)
    Includes bibliographical references and index.
    ISBN 978–0–7613–4222–9 (lib. bdg. : alk. paper)
    1. Sacagawea—Juvenile literature. 2. Shoshoni women—Biography—Juvenile
literature. 3. Shoshoni Indians—Biography—Juvenile literature. 4. Lewis and
Clark Expedition (1804–1806)—Juvenile literature. I. Title.
F592.7.S123S87 2009
978.004'9745740092—dc22 [B]   2008030638

Manufactured in the United States of America
1 2 3 4 5 6 – PA – 14 13 12 11 10 09

TABLE OF CONTENTS

INTRODUCTION 5

1. CAPTURED! 6

2. JOURNEY OF DISCOVERY 14

3. THESE ARE MY PEOPLE 21

4. TO THE OCEAN 28

5. JOURNEY'S END 36

TIMELINE 44

THERE IS MORE THAN ONE
WAY TO TELL A STORY 45

FURTHER READING 46

WEBSITES 46

SELECTED BIBLIOGRAPHY 47

INDEX 48

INTRODUCTION

Sacagawea was an ordinary girl who did something extraordinary. In 1805 and 1806, she accompanied Captains Lewis and Clark on their Journey of Discovery. Their job was to explore from the Missouri River all the way to the Pacific Ocean. This part of the country was still a mysterious wilderness to white Americans.

Sacagawea was a Shoshone Indian. She was brought along to be an interpreter for the captains. But she became much more. Her good sense and her courage won her the respect of the explorers. By the time she was a young woman, Sacagawea had earned a place in American history.

This is her story.

1 Captured!

The Shoshone girl's heart pounded as she ran. Behind her, she could hear the thunder of hoofbeats. Warriors were coming! Around her, friends and family scrambled to escape. The girl ran to the river. If she could get across, she might be safe.

At once, the girl felt herself being lifted up. Suddenly she was on horseback. A warrior's arms were tight around her. Then, just as suddenly, she was headed away from the river, away from her family, and away from her old life. Everything the girl had ever known was lost that day. Even her Shoshone name was left behind. Soon she would be called Sacagawea.

Sacagawea was born in about 1789 in the western Rocky Mountains. Later, white people would make that area part of Idaho. But no white people were there then. Her language did not even have a word for "white person."

Sacagawea was born in this area of the Rocky Mountains.

Herds of wild bison provided food, clothing, and shelter for Sacagawea's people. English speakers often called these animals buffalo.

The Shoshones did not stay in one place for very long. They moved often to gather wild plants or to hunt buffalo. As she grew, Sacagawea learned to look for tasty plants and roots to eat. She helped her mother set up the buffalo skin tepee that was the family's home.

When she was about eleven, the Shoshones camped at a place where three rivers came together. Then Hidatsa Indians came. They attacked the Shoshones. They captured Sacagawea and carried her off.

Sacagawea was taken five hundred miles away to the Hidatsa village. She was not quite a slave of the Hidatsa. But she was not free to leave, either. She was given the name Sacagawea, or Bird Woman: *tsakaka* for "bird," and *wias* for "woman." As the seasons passed, Sacagawea learned to speak the Hidatsa language. But she never forgot her days in the mountains. And she never forgot her Shoshone language.

Sacagawea was taken to a Hidatsa village in modern-day North Dakota. Artist George Catlin made this 1832 painting of the village as it appeared in 1810.

The village was on the Knife River, which flows into the larger Missouri River. Sometimes people from other Native American groups traveled the Missouri River to the village. White men came too. They were the first white men that Sacagawea had ever seen.

One was a fur trapper named Toussaint Charbonneau. Charbonneau lived in the village from time to time. He was much older than Sacagawea. Even so, he bought her from the Hidatsa and made her his wife. She was about fifteen.

THE PROUD "CHIEF"

Toussaint Charbonneau was a vain, boastful man. The Hidatsa treated him as a bit of a clown. They gave him mocking nicknames such as Chief of the Little Village and Great Horse from Afar.

Meriwether Lewis served as the personal secretary to President Thomas Jefferson before he became an explorer.

One day, other white men came. Captains Meriwether Lewis and William Clark were explorers. They were leading a group of men on a great journey. They were heading west, all the way to the Pacific Ocean. The captains hoped to go the whole way by boat, following the rivers to the sea.

The Hidatsa warned them that they would have to cross the mountains along the way. They would need horses to do that. The Shoshones live in the mountains, the Hidatsa said. They had many horses. Perhaps the captains could trade with them.

Winter was approaching quickly. The captains built a fort not far from the Hidatsa village. They stayed there while the river was frozen. Many people went to see the white men's fort. Charbonneau and Sacagawea went too.

Charbonneau offered to join the captains on their journey. He had spent many years among the Native American peoples along the river, he said. He could speak many of their languages. His wife, he added, could speak Shoshone.

William Clark (LEFT) met Lewis while both men were serving in the army in Ohio.

This painting shows the captains making plans with Charbonneau and Sacagawea at the Hidatsa village.

This was certainly good news! The captains knew they would need Charbonneau to help translate for them. But they were especially happy to have Sacagawea along. Their journey would depend on getting Shoshone horses to cross the mountains. And Sacagawea was the only one who could speak the Shoshone language.

If the journey was to succeed, it would be up to this teenage girl to speak for the captains.

2 JOURNEY OF DISCOVERY

Sacagawea had become a member of the team. Another member was to be added soon. Sacagawea was expecting a baby that winter. Since the captains were planning to leave in the spring, Sacagawea would have to carry her newborn baby with her on the journey.

Early that winter, Sacagawea and her husband moved into the captains' fort. Sacagawea waited for her baby to be born. The captains waited for the ice to leave the river.

Meanwhile, Sacagawea tried to get used to the white men. At Christmas, the men gave a big party. They shared a meal and fired their guns. One of the men played the fiddle. Sacagawea watched with amusement as these rough bearded men danced a square dance with one another.

Men dance to fiddle music at Lewis and Clark's Christmas party at the fort.

On February 11, 1805, Sacagawea's
waiting was over. The birth was not easy.
Captain Lewis wanted to help. He tried
giving her a very strange medicine: two rings
of a rattlesnake's rattle, broken into pieces
and mixed with water. It seemed to work.
Ten minutes later, Sacagawea was holding
her baby son. Charbonneau named the boy
Jean Baptiste. The friendly Captain Clark
nicknamed him Pompey, or Pomp for short.

Just eight weeks later, on April 7, 1805,
Sacagawea packed little Pompey into a
cradleboard. Then she
strapped the cradleboard
to her back. It was
time to leave.

Captain Lewis gave
Sacagawea rattlesnake
rattles like these.

York was the only African American on the journey.

Most of the explorers were soldiers. Another was an expert hunter. Captain Clark's slave, York, went along too. So did Captain Lewis's big black dog, Seaman. In all, thirty-three people left the fort for the journey up the Missouri River. Sacagawea was the only woman.

She knew just how to help. Each night, she helped York set up the buffalo skin tepee her family shared with the captains. She found berries and plants to eat. One day, she spotted a pile of driftwood. Sacagawea knew it was a place where mice had hidden tasty roots. The roots made a welcome addition to the meal that night.

Shoshone women carried
their babies in cradleboards
like this one.

On nice days, Sacagawea walked
along the shore. She carried little Pompey
bundled on her back. When he was hungry,
she nursed him. When he was wet, she put
fresh cattail fluff in his cradleboard. In the
evenings, she played with him by firelight.

Sometimes she rode in one of the large,
flat-bottomed canoes called pirogues. All
the captains' important papers, medicines,
and tools were packed into the pirogue
too. Once, when her husband was steering,
a sudden wind struck the boat. The boat
tipped and nearly overturned. Water began
to pour in. The captains' precious packages
began to float away.

The captains were walking onshore. They shouted orders to Charbonneau. The men shouted threats. Charbonneau just wailed in fear. Only Sacagawea stayed calm. She leaned out of the boat and scooped up books, papers, and whatever else she could reach. Finally, the boat was brought to shore. Sacagawea had saved nearly everything. The captains did not forget her help. A week later, they named a river Bird Woman's River in her honor.

After many weeks, the explorers came to a fork in the river. The Hidatsa had spoken of a great waterfall. But which way was it? The captains decided to split up to find out. Sacagawea stayed with Captain Clark.

The explorers camped at the fork in the river where the Marias and Missouri rivers meet.

Then she fell ill. For days, she burned with fever. Captain Clark gave her medicine. He cut her to make her bleed. At the time, people thought this would cure illness. She only grew weaker.

One morning, Captain Clark woke to find her much worse. He wrote in his journal, "Her case is somewhat dangerous." His worry showed in those few words. Sacagawea was dying.

SPELL IT RIGHT—SAY IT RIGHT

In their journals, the captains always spelled Sacagawea's name with a *g*. They pronounced it that way too: *sah-cah-gah-wee-ah*. Later, someone copied the captains' journals. By mistake, he spelled her name with a *j*. The mistake stuck. People have been getting Sacagawea's name wrong ever since.

3 THESE ARE MY PEOPLE

When Captain Lewis returned, he was alarmed. It was clear that Sacagawea was near death. What would happen to Pomp if she died? What would happen to them all? She was their only link to the Shoshones and horses. So much depended on this girl!

Then the captain remembered a spring he had seen not far away. The water from the spring was full of minerals. Perhaps it would help. He sent a man to bring him some of the water. After drinking it, Sacagawea felt stronger. Within a few days, she was well again.

The waterfall they were looking for turned out to be a series of *five* waterfalls. They had to go around on land. The canoes and all the baggage had to be carried.

The captain's spring still pours fresh water into the Missouri River. It is called Giant Springs.

The explorers had to carry their canoes and supplies around this waterfall and four others.

Sacagawea hiked around the falls with Pompey on her back. She carried his clothes and blankets in his cradleboard. One day, she walked through a narrow valley with her husband and Captain Clark. A storm caught them by surprise. Almost at once, the valley began to flood. Suddenly a wall of water and tumbling boulders was roaring toward them.

Charbonneau scrambled up a hill to safety. Sacagawea quickly pulled Pompey into her arms. Captain Clark helped push her up the hill. They were safe. But Pompey's cradleboard and all his clothes were lost.

Travelers carried boats and supplies over land. This is called portaging.

The climb around the falls took a month. That was much longer than anyone had counted on. By now it was July. They had to get across the mountains soon. Fall came early in the mountains. And with fall would come snow.

At times, the river flowed too swiftly to paddle the canoes. The men dragged the boats through the water. Onshore, the ground was a carpet of prickly cactus. The spines cut the travelers' feet right through their moccasins.

Then one morning, there was good news. Sacagawea saw familiar places. She showed the captains a spot where she had camped with her Shoshone family.

Days later, she came to a place she remembered very well. It was a place where three rivers came together. Sacagawea told the captains the story of her capture. She pointed to the place in the river where she had been taken. If it was hard for her to tell the story, she did not show it. She did not cry.

Sacagawea recognized this place as the site of her capture.

Sacagawea recognized this hill from her childhood with the Shoshones. It is shaped like a beaver's head.

Once, in the distance, she saw a rocky hill with an unusual shape. It looked something like the head of an animal. She knew that hill! The Shoshones called it Beaver's Head. Sacagawea told the captains that her people would be nearby.

It was not a moment too soon. The men were exhausted. They could go no farther. They had to have horses. But where were the Shoshones?

Captain Lewis decided he would go ahead to look. He took with him a man who knew the sign language used among Native Americans. Surely he would also take Sacagawea to speak the Shoshone language.

Instead, the captains asked Sacagawea only for the Shoshone word for "white man." Of course, since the Shoshones had never seen white people, there was none. So she gave them the closest word she could think of, "Ta-ba-bone." (The word really meant something like "stranger.")

For over a week, there was no sign of Lewis or the Shoshones. Then one morning, Sacagawea was walking with Captain Clark. She looked up to see men approaching on horseback. They were Shoshones with Captain Lewis! Sacagawea leaped with joy. Using motions, she told Captain Clark the good news: these are my people!

THE CAPTAINS' MYSTERY

Why did Lewis and his men leave behind the only person who could speak Shoshone? Perhaps they counted on using signs to communicate with the Shoshones at first. Off they went with only one Shoshone word. If they met the Shoshone people, they could only wave their arms and yell the word for "stranger."

4 To THE Ocean

Home! Sacagawea was home! Captain Lewis had found the Shoshone people. For the first time in five years, Sacagawea saw the familiar faces of her childhood.

A girl ran out from the crowd. She threw her arms around Sacagawea. She was Sacagawea's old friend. She had been with Sacagawea on the day of the Hidatsa attack. The girls hugged and laughed and cried.

Sacagawea rushed to greet her childhood friend.

Late that afternoon, it was time for the meeting between the captains and the Shoshone chief. Sacagawea was called upon to translate. Charbonneau was there too. So was one of the soldiers, who spoke French.

The chief would speak in Shoshone to Sacagawea. She would translate the Shoshone into Hidatsa for Charbonneau. Then Charbonneau was to translate the Hidatsa into French for the soldier. Finally, the soldier would translate the French into English for the captains. Every question had to go through a chain of five people. Every answer went back through the chain the other way.

But when the chief began to speak, Sacagawea stared. That voice! It was a voice from her past. Then she knew. The chief was her brother!

At once, Sacagawea jumped up. She hugged her brother and cried over him. She wrapped her blanket around him, a warm Shoshone gesture of love.

Sacagawea introduced Pompey to her brother, the Shoshone chief.

A Native American gave this piece of shell jewelry to one of the captains on the journey. It may have been a gift from the Shoshones, who prized shells from the distant ocean.

In the days that followed, Sacagawea visited with her Shoshone family and friends. She translated for the captains as they traded for horses. She helped them find guides to lead them through the mountains. The captains were eager to get started. Already they could see their breath in the morning air.

All too soon, it was time for Sacagawea to leave. The baggage was packed onto the horses. The canoes were left behind.

On September 1, 1805, the explorers set out. They followed a Shoshone guide. Before them rose the terrible snow-covered Rocky Mountains. It was not a welcoming sight.

For eleven days, Sacagawea and the men struggled over the rough and rocky trails. The horses slipped and crashed down the steep mountainsides. It rained, hailed, and snowed, sometimes all in one day.

Worst of all, the food ran out. Some days, there was not so much as a rabbit to catch for supper. The hungry men killed and ate two of the horses. Sacagawea refused. The Shoshones did not eat horsemeat. Her stomach rumbled day and night.

SACAGAWEA'S MYSTERY

Why didn't Sacagawea stay with her Shoshone friends and family? Why did she leave with the captains? No one knows. If she had thoughts of staying, she never told the captains.

The captains met with the Nez Perce, who agreed to take care of the party's horses.

At last, the explorers stumbled out of the mountains. Still, their work was not done. The exhausted men had to make new canoes to continue the journey. The horses were left with the friendly Nez Perce Indians for safekeeping.

Once more, Sacagawea was traveling by boat. But the rivers flowing from the mountains were swift. The water was full of rapids and rocks. She kept a tight hold on little Pomp in the canoe.

Captain Lewis sketched these pictures of the expedition's canoes in his journal.

Sometimes the riverbanks were crowded with Native Americans fishing for salmon. Some were frightened by the strange white men in canoes. But seeing Sacagawea put them at ease. They knew that no war party would bring a woman and a baby along.

The days grew shorter. Everywhere there were signs that the explorers were nearing the ocean. The river rose and fell with the tides. Sacagawea could taste the ocean's salt in the river water.

Once Captain Clark saw what he thought was the ocean in the distance. But it was only the river as it widened on its way to the sea.

That night, though, Sacagawea heard a sound she had never heard before. It was the roar of waves crashing against rocks. The men heard it too. Throughout the camp, spirits soared. It was the Pacific! The ocean was within reach!

Captain Clark thought he spied the Pacific through his telesope.

5 JOURNEY'S END

Hearing the ocean was one thing. Getting there was something else.

For a week, the explorers tried to reach the Pacific by boat. Wind and waves kept pushing them back. The captains took turns hiking to the ocean. Finally, they decided the boats would go no farther. Winter was nearing. They would have to build a fort to spend the winter.

But where was the best place for the fort? The captains put it to a vote. Everyone, even York and Sacagawea, got a say. Sacagawea voted for a place where there were plenty of roots to eat. With her words, she became the first woman in American history to cast a vote.

In the end, they chose a spot a few miles from the ocean. They built seven cabins and a tall fence surrounding them. Sacagawea and her family had their own little hut. The group named the camp Fort Clatsop, after the friendly Clatsop Indians who lived nearby.

Captain Clark traced this plan of Fort Clatsop on the cover of his journal. The fort had seven cabins, each with a central fireplace. The gate to the fort is on the left.

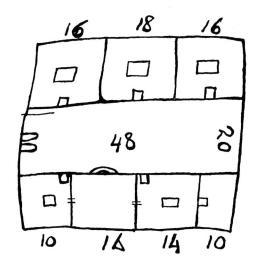

One day, there was exciting news in camp. A whale had washed up on the beach. Captain Clark and some of the men made plans to go see the enormous animal. Sacagawea wanted to go too. It would be her first chance to see the ocean. But she was told she was to stay behind.

Sacagawea almost never disagreed with the captains. But this was too much! She had traveled a long way to see the great waters, she said firmly. And there was even a "monstrous fish" to be seen. It wasn't fair that she was not allowed to see either one. Of course, the captains had to agree. Sacagawea got to see the whale.

Many Native Americans came to harvest the whale's meat. American artist George Catlin witnessed a similar scene fifty years later and recorded it in this painting.

Researchers built this replica of Fort Clatsop using Clark's plans. The fort was only about fifty feet long.

The winter at Fort Clatsop was long, rainy, and miserable. The wet weather made everyone grumpy. Clothes and blankets rotted. Food spoiled.

By spring, everyone had had enough. They waited for a dry day to start their return trip. On March 23, 1806, Sacagawea packed her family's few belongings and said good-bye to Fort Clatsop.

Sacagawea (CENTER) stands with Pompey near a fire in the explorers' camp not far from the Nez Perce village.

The explorers set out the way they had come. By May, they had reached the Rocky Mountains once more. They collected their horses from the Nez Perces. Then they waited for the snow to melt. Each of them remembered very well the struggle to cross the mountains the year before. But this time, they were luckier. Once enough snow had melted, the crossing took only six days.

The captains decided to split up. Captain Lewis and some of the men would explore a river to the north. Sacagawea and her family went with Captain Clark and the others. They would head toward the Yellowstone River to the south.

Just a few days after starting out, though, the trail scattered in every direction. Clark didn't know which way to go. But Sacagawea did. She had been there many times as a child. She pointed the way.

A week later, she told him about a shortcut through the mountains to the river. Captain Clark was happy to take her advice. In his journal, he wrote that Sacagawea "has been of great service to me as a pilot through this country."

Sacagawea led Captain Clark through this mountain pass near modern Bozeman, Montana.

On August 12, the party met Captain Lewis again. Two days later, the Hidatsa village was in sight. Sacagawea was back where she had started. To the Pacific Ocean and back, she had traveled more than 4,300 miles.

Sacagawea's grand adventure was over. Captains Lewis and Clark said good-bye and continued their return trip. The captains took with them the journals they had written along the way. The journals told the story of all that had happened on the Journey of Discovery.

They told Sacagawea's story too. In time, the American people would read the journals. They would come to know Sacagawea's name. They would see that this young Shoshone woman had helped to make the captains' journey a success.

Captain Clark filled this and several other journals with notes on the journey.

SMALL PAY FOR A BIG JOB

For his work on the journey, Charbonneau was paid five hundred dollars. Sacagawea received nothing but the captains' thanks.

After the expedition, Sacagawea did not stay in the Hidatsa village. She did not go back to the Shoshones either. She never saw her Shoshone family or friends again.

By 1812, the family had moved to Fort Manuel in present-day South Dakota. That December, Sacagawea fell ill and died. She was about twenty-three. She left behind Pompey and a baby girl named Lizette. After her death, Captain Clark cared for both her children. (Her husband continued to work as a fur trader.)

A clerk at the fort recorded Sacagawea's death in his journal. Perhaps his words sum her up best: "She was a good [woman] and the best woman in the fort."

TIMELINE

In the year . . .

1800 Sacagawea was captured by the Hidatsa.   Age 11

1801 Thomas Jefferson became the third president of the United States.

1803 Jefferson chose Meriwether Lewis to lead an expedition to the Pacific Ocean. Lewis asked William Clark to join him.

1804 Sacagawea married Toussaint Charbonneau.   Age 15

Lewis and Clark began their Journey of Discovery in May.

Sacagawea and Charbonneau became part of the expedition in November.

1805 Pompey was born in February.

Sacagawea began her journey with Lewis and Clark in April.

she became sick in June.

she was reunited with the Shoshones in August.

1806 she saw the Pacific Ocean for the first time in January.   Age 17

she left Fort Clatsop in March.

she returned to the Hidatsa village in August.

1812 her daughter Lizette was born.

Sacagawea died on December 20.   Age 23

THERE IS MORE THAN ONE WAY TO TELL A STORY

The Hidatsa and Shoshone people tell their own stories of Sacagawea. Their stories are not written down. They are spoken tales, handed down from old to young.

Hidatsa children learn that Sacagawea was not Shoshone at all. She and her brother were Hidatsa. They were captured by the Shoshones and taken to the mountains. They learned to speak the Shoshone language. In time, Sacagawea made her way back to the Hidatsa village. Her brother, though, stayed behind to become a Shoshone chief.

According to Shoshone legend, Sacagawea did not die as a young woman. Instead, she left her husband. Over time, she lived with several different Native American groups. Later, she returned to the Shoshone people and became a wise and powerful leader. She died an old, old woman, loved and respected by her people.

This statue of Sacagawea and Pompey stands in Bismarck, North Dakota.

45

FURTHER READING

Erdrich, Lise. *Sacagawea.* **Minneapolis: Carolrhoda Books, 2003.** Illustrations by Julie Buffalohead bring Sacagawea to life in this picture-book biography.

Hunsaker, Joyce Badgley. *Sacagawea Speaks: Beyond the Shining Mountains with Lewis and Clark.* **Guilford, CT: Two Dot Books, 2001.** This tells Sacagawea's story as she might have told it herself, with photos of the animals, plants, and places she would have seen on her journey. For older readers.

Pringle, Laurence. *American Slave, American Hero: York of the Lewis and Clark Expedition.* **Honesdale, PA: Calkins Creek Books, 2005.** Read the story of Captain Clark's slave, York, and his role on the Journey of Discovery.

Ransom, Candice. *Lewis and Clark.* **Minneapolis: Lerner Publications Company, 2003.** This biography of both captains explores how they met, their famous expedition, and their lives after the journey.

WEBSITES

Corps of Discovery—Sacagawea
http://www.nps.gov/archive/jeff/LewisClark2/ CorpsofDiscovery/TheOthers/Civilians/Sacagawea.htm This biography of Sacagawea includes interesting facts about her name, her role on the journey, and her life as a Hidatsa.

History of the Sacagawea Dollar
http://www.coinfacts.com/historical_notes/history_of_the _sacagawea_dollar.htm Find out how Sacagawea was chosen in 1999 to appear on the U.S. mint's golden dollar coin.

Lewis and Clark: Inside the Corps
http://www.pbs.org/lewisandclark/inside/index.html
This website includes biographies of every member of the
expedition, including Sacagawea, from the captains to
Lewis's dog, Seaman.

Lewis and Clark's Historic Trail
http://www.lewisclark.net/index.html This site includes
maps, a timeline, and quirky facts about the Journey of
Discovery.

SELECTED BIBLIOGRAPHY

Ambrose, Stephen. *Undaunted Courage: Meriwether Lewis,
Thomas Jefferson, and the Opening of the American
West.* New York: Simon and Schuster, 1996.

Bergon, Frank, ed. *The Journals of Lewis and Clark.* New
York: Viking, 1989.

Clark, Ella E., and Margot Edmonds. *Sacagawea of the
Lewis and Clark Expedition.* Berkeley: University of
California Press, 1979.

Gilman, Carolyn, and Mary Jane Schneider. *The Way to
Independence: Memories of a Hidatsa Indian Family,
1840–1920.* Saint Paul: Minnesota Historical Society
Press, 1987.

Luttig, John C. *Journal of a Fur-Trading Expedition on the
Upper Missouri, 1812–1813.* Edited by Stella M. Drumm.
Saint Louis: Missouri Historical Society, 1920.

Trenholm, Virginia Cole, and Maurine Carley. *The
Shoshonis: Sentinels of the Rockies.* Norman: University
of Oklahoma Press, 1964.

INDEX

brother, 30

buffalo, 8

capture, 8–9, 25

Charbonneau, Jean Baptiste "Pompey" (son), 14, 16, 18, 23, 33

Charbonneau, Toussaint (husband), 10, 19, 23; as translator, 12–13, 29

Clark, William, 11, 12, 20, 23, 27, 35, 43; journal of, 37, 41, 42

death, 43

Fort Clatsop, 37, 39

Hidatsa, 8–9, 11, 19, 45

hunger, 32

Journey of Discovery, 5, 11, 42

Lewis, Meriwether, 11, 21, 26–27; journal of, 34

Missouri River, 10, 25

Nez Perce, 33, 40

Pacific Ocean, 35

pirogue (canoe), 18, 34

Rocky Mountains, 7, 40

Shoshone, 8–9, 11, 26–27, 45; Sacagawea's reunion, 28–31

sickness, 20–22

whale, 38

Yellowstone River, 40

York, 17

Acknowledgments

For photographs and artwork: The images in this book are used with the permission of: © Connie Ricca/CORBIS, p. 4; © Macduff Everton/The Image Bank/Getty Images, p. 7; © Sam Lund/Independent Picture Service, p. 8; © Smithsonian American Art Museum, Washington, DC/Art Resource, NY, p. 9; Independence National Historical Park, pp. 11, 12; State Historical Society of North Dakota, p. 13; © Washington State Historical Society/Art Resource, NY, pp. 15, 33, 35, 40; © 2002 Missouri Historical Society, St. Louis, 1953 129 0033, photograph by Melinda Muirhead, NS 26101, p. 16; © Michael Haynes - www.mhaynesart.com, pp. 17, 30; © President and Fellows of Harvard University,Peabody Museum, 99-12-10/53016, p. 18; © Nancy Carter/North Wind Picture Archives, pp. 19, 25, 41; © Sunpix Travel/Alamy, p. 22; © De Agostini Picture Library/G. Sioen/Getty Images, p. 23; © North Wind Picture Archives, pp. 24, 37; © Marilyn Angel Wynn/Nativestock.com/Getty Images, p. 26; William Henry Jackson Collection/Scotts Bluff National Monument, p. 29; University of Pennsylvania Museum of Archeology and Anthropology, object L-83-4 a, b, image #152320, p. 31; American Philosophical Society, p. 34; George Catlin, *A Whale Ashore-Klahoquat* (detail), Paul Mellon Collection, image courtesy of the Board of Trustees, National Gallery of Art, Washington, DC, p. 38; Lewis and Clark National Historical Park, National Park Service, p. 39; © 2002 Missouri Historical Society Archives, St. Louis, photograph by Cary Horton. NS 26081, p. 42; © Visions of America/Joe Sohm/Digital Vision/Getty Images, p. 45. Front cover: © Michael Haynes - www.mhaynesart.com. Back cover: Collection of the Jackson Hole Historical Society and Museum, 1991.0087.032.

For quoted material: p. 20, Frank Bergon, ed., *The Journals of Lewis and Clark* (New York: Viking, 1989), 167; p. 27, Bergon, 223; p. 38, Bergon, 341; p. 41, Bergon, 443; p. 43, John C. Luttig, *Journal of a Fur-Trading Expedition on the Upper Missouri, 1812–1813* (Saint Louis: Missouri Historical Society, 1920), 106.